God Is Good: A Lecture

George Shaw Cook

In the interest of creating a more extensive selection of rare historical book reprints, we have chosen to reproduce this title even though it may possibly have occasional imperfections such as missing and blurred pages, missing text, poor pictures, markings, dark backgrounds and other reproduction issues beyond our control. Because this work is culturally important, we have made it available as a part of our commitment to protecting, preserving and promoting the world's literature. Thank you for your understanding.

GOD IS GOOD

A LECTURE DELIVERED BY

GEORGE SHAW COOK, C.S.B.

AS A MEMBER OF THE BOARD OF LECTURESHIP OF
THE FIRST CHURCH OF CHRIST, SCIENTIST,
IN BOSTON, MASSACHUSETTS

THE CHRISTIAN SCIENCE PUBLISHING SOCIETY
FALMOUTH AND ST. PAUL STREETS
BOSTON, MASSACHUSETTS
U. S. A.

BX6945
C6

Copyright, 1917, by
The Christian Science Publishing Society.

GOD IS GOOD

UPON first hearing of Christian Science one will very naturally inquire: What does it promise to do for me? Does it promise to heal me of disease and to save me from sin? Will it give surcease to my sorrow and lift from me the burden of care? Can it break for me the spell of poverty, limitation, and fear? Is it able to say to the seething waves of mortal tumult, "Be still"?

PROMISES AND THEIR FULFILMENT

Those who have become acquainted with Christian Science in its application to human needs are able to assure the inquirer that it does all of this, and more. Unnumbered thousands are bearing grateful witness to the fact that they have felt the beneficent touch of Christian Science in their lives, and because of it they are being redeemed from the ills to which flesh is heir. Weekly in the Wednesday evening meetings of Christian Science churches testimony is being given to the healing and redemptive power of Christian Science. Month after month and year after year a never ending, uninterrupted stream of reliable evidence of the healing power of Truth is going out to the world through the Christian Science periodicals. In these and in other ways the suffering, the sinning, and the sorrowing are coming to know that there is "balm in Gilead."

Unmistakable and irrefutable proof is to be found on every hand of the power of spiritual truth to destroy human error. Any earnest seeker may with comparatively little effort learn that through Christian Science his fellow men have been thoroughly and permanently healed of chronic and acute disease by spiritual means without the use of material remedies. He will learn as the result of investigation that these cases of healing by scientific mental treatment include many diseases ordinarily considered incurable. He will find that those numbered among the beneficiaries of Christian Science have been healed not merely of so-called functional and nervous troubles, but in many instances of those considered organic. He will ascertain that frequently these cases have been pronounced organic and incurable by reputable physicians, but that notwithstanding such pronouncement they have been healed perfectly, and often quickly, by Christian Science treatment. He will find that sometimes physicians are quite willing to give Christian Science credit for these marvelous cures.

The investigator will also learn that through Christian Science many have been rescued from lives of sin and vice, and that some have been lifted from the very depths of degradation and depravity. He will find that these persons have been restored to their rightful heritage of freedom from evil, and have thus become useful members of society. The seeker for facts concerning the effect of Christian Science in human experience will find that many who were not able to succeed in the struggle for existence, believing themselves to be the victims of environment and circumstances resulting in poverty and distress, are now finding their condition greatly improved because Christian Science has given them a new outlook on the world and a new insight into spiritual truth. He will find those who are glad to acknowledge that Christian Science has shown them how to be more honest, just, humble, loving, considerate—in a word, less selfish—than formerly. He will be told that the depressing atmosphere of discouragement and doubt has for many been transformed into an invigorating sense of courage and confidence.

MEANS OF DELIVERANCE

If the investigator were to inquire how all this came to pass, and could have a concrete answer from all the Christian Scientists on earth, that answer would be, It is because we have come to know that God is good. A simple answer, is it not?—and yet no more simple and scarcely less profound than the declaration of the apostle John that "God is love." If, as John says, "God is love," then God must also be infinitely good; for if we agree that God is infinite Love, surely we shall agree that infinite, universal, divine Love is identical with all that is good.

Christian Science teaches that God is not both good and evil, but that He is good only. Therefore God as understood in Christian Science is all good, and always good. He is never anything else than good, nor ever anything less than infinite. So as a basis for our discussion of Christian Science in some of its phases, we have the fundamental proposition that God is good, not merely in a relative sense, but always and forever immutably and perfectly good.

God is also described with equal correctness by the terms Spirit, Life, Truth, and by the word already used, Love. Likewise we may properly refer to God as infinite Mind, or Principle. Each of these terms conveys a different shade of meaning. All taken together serve to enlarge our conception of Deity. It will be seen that that which is infinitely good is also loving, tender, steadfast, merciful, and "unutterably kind" (Miscellaneous Writings, p. 312). That which is Love itself must be not only loving and good, but impartial, universal, changeless, and enduring. That which is Life, the only creative Principle, is not only good and loving, but also eternal, indestructible, incorruptible, changeless, self-existent. That which is infinite Truth, Spirit, or Mind, is not only good, loving, and eternal, but must also be conscious, active, omnipotent, and omniscient. Thus through using some of these definitions of God and of His qualities or attributes, we find that we have greatly amplified our sense of God. Not that words can adequately describe the infinite and eternal, not that the employment of terms or phrases can change God; but the proper use of these terms can help us better to comprehend the divine nature.

GOOD IS INFINITE

According to Christian Science this infinite God, divine Love, eternal Life, incorporeal Spirit or Mind, is the first and only cause or creator. Since there is but one cause, which is infinite and good, there can be but one kind of effect or manifestation, which must also be good and infinite. As the effect or manifestation of a creator that is infinite Spirit, or Mind, we can have as creation nothing less than the sum total of those spiritual ideas that express their divine origin. Therefore we learn in Christian Science that the only real, enduring, indestructible universe is mental or spiritual, and exists as the result or effect of the one infinitely good cause. This throws new light on the Scriptural declarations that God made all "that was made," and "God saw every thing that he had made, and, behold, it was very good."

The universal, complete expression of divine Mind, comprising all that exists by way of creation, necessarily includes individual spiritual man. This man reflects perfectly the infinite being called God. And this statement accords with the description of creation in the first chapter of Genesis, which says that God made man in "his own image" and after His likeness. If God made man in His image, it is certain that man must be exactly like his creator. When we recall that the one only cause is divine Mind, Spirit, Life, Love, then we see that man in the image of his creator must be spiritual, eternal, loving, and good, like his divine Principle.

Reviewing our discussion from this point, we see that we have, first, a perfectly good God who is infinite Spirit, or Mind. Next, we have a perfectly good universe which is spiritual or mental, and consists of those ideas that are good and true. Then we have a perfectly good man included in this spiritual universe as the reflection or image of his infinite Father-Mother, divine Mind.

But, you say, what of a material universe and mortal man? What of the existence into which mortals seem to have been born and out of which they appear to pass into an uncertain and indefinite future state? What of sin and suffering and sickness and death? What of evil, and matter?. We shall not ignore them, although we have already seen why in the best sense they cannot be real, for the simple reason that they are not good. No one believes that evil is good, although he may try to make himself believe that in some way it has been provided for his benefit. We have begun with a good cause, which made all "that was made." Effect must be like cause. Evil is not like good. Matter is not like Spirit. Therefore evil and matter cannot reasonably be attributed to the one good, spiritual cause.

UNREALITY OF EVIL

Christian Science, in explaining the unreal nature of evil, first declares that matter, being non-intelligent, cannot be conscious of evil. It cannot of itself sin or have the impulse to sin. It cannot be hateful, dishonest, or afraid. What, then, sins? God cannot behold or look upon evil or iniquity; He cannot have created evil, therefore He cannot know or be conscious of it. Christian Science consequently makes the positive assertion that evil, being utterly opposed to good and totally unlike good, does not exist in God or as the manifestation or effect of God. Christian Scientists do not, however, ignore the claim of sin to exist as a part of human experience. They understand that in this sense it must be recognized as a false claim, to be repented of and forsaken before it can be demonstrated to be what it really is—nothing. They understand that the scientific forsaking of sin and its forgiveness, or destruction, comes through Christ, the true, spiritual idea of God as being of "purer eyes than to behold evil."

UNREALITY OF MATTER

Closely associated with the thought of evil is the thought of matter. Indeed, they cannot be dissociated. Where one is, the other will always be found. Mrs. Eddy's teaching that matter is unreal, and that what appears to be material substance is but the concept of the human mind, is slowly but surely being recognized by material scientists to be correct. It has been said of what is called matter that it is "a suppositional vacuum in a hypothetical medium." This "hypothetical medium" is known as ether, of which it has been recently written by Edgar Lucien Larkin, "The most refined experiments ever made, those by Michelson, failed utterly to detect the existence of ether." Rather indefinite and unsatisfactory as a medium, is it not?

A noted Englishman, Mr. Balfour, at the London Congress of the Natural Scientists of Great Britain, is credited with having said, "The material sciences are now explaining matter by explaining it away." Those who have explained matter away, leaving nothing in its place but an indefinite hypothesis, have not done as well as Mrs. Eddy, the Discoverer and Founder of Christian Science, for she has explained the unreality of matter and of its supposed cause by revealing the one infinite, indivisible substance to be divine Mind and its ideas. (See Science and Health, p. 468.)

We seem to exist in matter bodies which are part of a material universe. But what dependence may we place on the five physical senses which alone testify to the reality of this existence? At best the testimony of the physical senses is faulty and unreliable. Many familiar illustrations of the unreliability of sense-testimony could be cited. Every one knows that the sense of taste is deceptive and sometimes makes very cold things seem hot. The sense of hearing often seems to make sound originate in some place where it does not. To illustrate the deceptive nature of the sense of touch, one need only cross the second finger over the index finger, and after closing his eyes roll a pencil or small round object on a flat surface. There will appear to be two of these objects instead of one, if the sense-testimony is left uncorrected.

If these senses cannot testify truly of material things, how can they be expected to give reliable evidence regarding those things which are spiritual and eternal? As a matter of fact, the physical senses have no higher conception of reality than that which can be weighed and measured, whereas spiritual sense recognizes as substance only that which is imponderable and infinite.

Beginning with the objective universe, many philosophers, reasoning inductively from effect back to cause, ultimately arrive by way of atoms, ions, or electrons, at what they call force or energy. Mrs. Eddy attributes to what she terms "mortal mind" all that seems to be material, evil, and mortal. This term "mortal mind" is used by Mrs. Eddy as the best term available to describe the false sense of intelligence and life that claims to exist as the antipode of God. But she explains that the real Mind and creator is not mortal, but immortal; not human, but divine. Thus the world of sense-perception is left without a divine cause. The troublesome thing called matter is left outside the realm of divine reality; it is found to have no real authority and no enduring substance. Of this fleeting, temporary sense of substance Paul said, "The things which are seen are temporal; but the things which are not seen are eternal."

PAIN AND SUFFERING ILLUSIVE

Because the mortal, material body is not conscious, it cannot, apart from the human mind, be painful or sore or sick. The human body separate from the human mind can have no sensation. It is obvious, then, that the sense of pain and suffering is in the human mind and not in the body. Many have doubtless had the experience of dreaming that they were in pain when the body was in what is regarded as a normal state. Christian Science shows that all suffering and disease is a dream from which the dreamer needs to be awakened. The first step in the direction of freedom from this evil dream of disease and mortality is to know that these evils are not of God. God never made anything that is not good. Furthermore God, being always good, cannot make use of evil for any purpose or tolerate its existence in any form.

The Christian Scientist is willing to admit that suffering and disease seem to exist and that matter often seems quite real and very painful. He does not deny that to human sense this is so, but seeks to correct this false sense of things with the truth of being.

He finds that by letting that Mind be in him "which was also in Christ Jesus," thereby substituting in consciousness ideas that are good for beliefs that are evil, he can free himself from the sense of pain and suffering, which is called sickness, as surely as he can by a similar mental process resist and overcome the temptation to sin. Evil, pain, and disease are without divine authority or actual existence, and cannot even seem to exist to one who is fully conscious of the allness and ever-presence of good.

DISEASE UNLAWFUL

The question is sometimes asked, Since the Bible contains a record of human suffering, why does Christian Science, which is said to be founded upon the Scriptures, teach that suffering should be opposed?

Christian Science is a restoration or rediscovery of primitive Christianity. It is based upon the life and works of Christ Jesus, who was the Founder of Christianity. Christian Science, therefore, accepts Jesus as the master Christian. The question arises, What was the attitude of Christ Jesus toward human suffering? A study of the gospels reveals the fact that while the attitude of Jesus toward the sufferer was one of great compassion, he evidently regarded suffering and disease as illegitimate. He declared that he came not to destroy, but to fulfil. He came, in other words, to do the will of the Father, God. We find that much of the ministry of Jesus consisted in his work of destroying sickness, suffering, sin, and death. If Christ Jesus came to do the will of God, and spent his time largely in relieving mankind through the destruction of disease as well as of sin, then it can only be concluded that he regarded suffering as unlawful and contrary to the will of God.

Furthermore, Jesus said, "Ye shall know the truth, and the truth shall make you free." The question occurs, Free from what? The answer is again found in the record of his works among men. It is recorded that he "went about doing good," and "healing all manner of sickness and all manner of disease among the people." The conclusion again is that if the truth as taught by Christ Jesus makes free from sickness and disease, then these evils are the opposite of truth, and should be opposed and cast out as being no part of the purpose and plan of God for man, who is created in His likeness. Christian Science teaches that the works of Jesus were done in accordance with divine law. It teaches, therefore, that the same works can be done again in the same way, for real law never varies in its operation.

DISEASE HAS A MENTAL CAUSE

What of the experience called sickness, or disease? Practically all are familiar with the fact recognized and admitted by physicians, that certain kinds of disease have a mental cause. Christian Science declares that all disease has a mental cause.

Human emotions, such as fear, anger, worry, hatred, etc., are now said to produce poisonous conditions on or in the physical body. If this is so, may not many cases of chronic poisoning in the human system be traceable to a chronic disposition to give way to the emotions? Is it not as reasonable to admit this as to recognize the fact that acute fear immediately manifests itself in a blanched face? If one is obliged to admit the mental cause of some kinds of physical disease, why not agree with Christian Science that, primarily, all disease is due to a mental cause? This does not mean that all disease is the result of conscious fear or of wilful sin. Many types of disease are effects of latent fear, hereditary temperament, superstition, ignorance, or some of the generally accepted beliefs of the human mind which seem to operate as law. Suppose a man to be sick from one or more of these mental causes. Will drugs cure him? Is there any antitoxin that will destroy hatred or any serum that will prevent fear? Nothing but

GOD IS GOOD 17

the knowledge that God is Love, and that man as the image of God is in reality nothing less than the expression of Love, and therefore can not and does not fear or hate, will effect a permanent cure in such a case.

FEAR OVERCOME

All that is real exists as the effect of an intelligent cause, divine Mind. One has only to look at a badly frightened person to see that he manifests little or no intelligence while under the sway of fear. Therefore we may conclude that fear is not the manifestation of an intelligent cause. It is plain that if one could be freed from fear it would be greatly to his advantage. Many are ready to point out the evil effects of fear. They are even quite ready to urge their friends not to be afraid, but they are not always able to tell them why they have no need to fear.

Christian Scientists having discerned the fact that fear is not an attribute of God, are beginning to understand why it is no part of man, who is in the likeness of God. They reason that God is the only cause and is good. Fear is not good. Therefore it is not the effect of the one only cause and consequently is without actual existence. There is no fear in the universe of God and nothing in that universe of which man could be afraid. There is no good in fear, for "fear hath torment;" hence there is no God in it, and no truth in it. Christian Scientists do not, however, claim to have demonstrated as yet that they are entirely immune from fear; but they are much less fearful than formerly, and consequently much less subject to disease and disaster.

HEREDITY NOT LAW

No more discouraging and distressing thought confronts mankind than the belief in hereditary transmission of disease or of certain evil tendencies and traits. When the so-called law of heredity seems to have resulted in a vigorous constitution and relatively good traits of mind and character, we are apt to rejoice that the individual has derived these from his progenitors; but when the inheritance is that of diseased physique or evil mentality, there is regret and despair in place of rejoicing.

If we are to admit that good tendencies can be transmitted by heredity, we shall also be obliged to admit that evil is likewise transmissible. But Mrs. Eddy has freed thousands from bondage to belief in hereditary transmission by her teaching that "heredity is not a law" (Science and Health, p. 178). Christian Science teaches, as Jesus taught, that God is the only Father of man. It shows that in his true nature man is the offspring of Spirit. Man's origin being divine Mind, and that Mind being infinitely good, man can have no evil heritage. His heritage is the heritage of good, and of good only. He is therefore not subject to hereditary taint or contamination. Purity and perfection are man's divine right and are derived from his heavenly Father. Today in many instances Christian Science is healing so-called hereditary diseases and congenital defects through the understanding that there is no law of God to sustain them, and that therefore they have no right to exist.

MAN-MADE LAWS NOT GOOD

The entire category of beliefs—such, for example, as those that claim to control the effect of food, climate, contagion, and many other generally accepted beliefs—are being proved not to be real law. The understanding that God is the only lawmaker shows at once that so-called material laws, not being of His ordaining, have no divine authority and no real power over man. Take the question of climatic influence: Christian Science teaches that it is not the weather but the belief about it that makes climate either injurious or otherwise. Consequently it shows that only right thinking will change wrong believing and free one from fear of climate or of its supposed effects.

Mrs. Eddy once treated a woman who breathed with difficulty when the wind was in the east. After treating her a few moments the breathing became natural. The wind, however, continued to blow directly from the east. (See Science and Health, p. 184.) This proves that it was not the direction of the wind but the belief about it that had made this woman's breathing difficult before she was relieved by Christian Science treatment. It is evident that such changes take place in consciousness, and that the mental process which substitutes the correct idea for the mistaken belief and its supposed penalty is not at all affected by the state of the weather. This tends to show that real atmosphere is mental, or spiritual, as was indicated by Paul when he said, "For in him [Spirit or Mind] we live, and move, and have our being."

The beliefs about infection and contagion are constantly changing, but practically all physicians agree that a calm and fearless state of thought is a great protection to the individual in times of epidemic or threatened epidemic of disease. Dr. Robert Collyer, the celebrated Unitarian minister, writing of his childhood experience and of his parents, said: "The most woeful fevers would break out in the cottages all about us, and decimate the neighbors, and they [his parents] were always at hand to help, going and coming as the sunshine goes and comes, never thinking of changing their garments. Yet they never caught a fever, nor did any of their children, nor felt the slightest touch of fear."

HEALTH IS UNIVERSAL

It should be understood that the best "health insurance" one can have is real presence of Mind, or the God-given ability to think truly at all times and under all circumstances.

Health, according to Christian Science, is universal. It is mental wholeness or completeness. It is spiritual perfection. It is reflected by the individual. It does not originate with him, nor does it belong to one more than to another. It is like the light—impersonal and universal. For one to have it does not prevent all from sharing it.

Real wealth, or true substance, is not only universal but indivisible. For one to possess it does not make it necessary or possible that others should be deprived of it. Even in daily experience it is seen, from a purely human point of view, that those qualities or characteristics which make for true success are intelligent activity, faithful persistence, courage, honesty, fidelity, etc. Christian Science shows that these qualities, if enduring, are not personal, but on the contrary are attributes of the one infinite Mind, or God. Therefore they are universal and may be reflected and manifested by all. Thus all may be conscious of the only enduring substance, and to be conscious of its ever-presence is to reflect and manifest divine Love, which, Mrs. Eddy says, "is impartial and universal in its adaptation and bestowals" (Science and Health, p. 13). So real wealth, or abundance, is as free as the sunshine and as universally available as truth. But the human sense of substance has often been that which is finite and divisible—that which may be bought and sold, borrowed, leased, and lost. One of our great American poets, discriminating between the false and true sense of substance, said:—

> At the devil's booth all things are sold,
> Each ounce of dross costs its ounce of gold;
> For a cap and bells our lives we pay,
> Bubbles we buy with a whole soul's tasking;
> 'Tis heaven alone that is given away,
> 'Tis only God may be had for the asking.

Christ Jesus, while understanding the universal nature of good and that man as the son of God is eternally supplied with all good, nevertheless recognized that mankind needs food and raiment. But in pointing the true way to find sufficient for temporal needs he said, "Seek ye first the kingdom of God, and his righteousness; and all these things shall be added unto you." Right thinking brings a sense of abundance today as surely as it did two thousand years ago. It is well, however, to remember that Jesus did not say to seek first the things, and the kingdom of God would be added.

Frequently students of the gospels fail to make any distinction between the terms Christ and Jesus. They often consider these terms as being synonymous. Christ is the spiritual, eternal, changeless, universal truth of God, which has been discerned to a greater or less extent in all ages, but which appeared in its perfection as an individual ideal in Christ Jesus. As the one who best understood and most perfectly demonstrated the Christ, Truth, in healing sickness and sin, Jesus was the Wayshower and Exemplar for mankind.

PRAYER AND ATONEMENT

Christian Science teaches its adherents to "pray without ceasing," and constantly to seek a higher and better understanding of the true nature of God, and of man as His likeness. Furthermore, it requires the demonstration of this understanding in right thinking and right living. Such thinking results in the lessening of sin and disease. This is the practical atonement to which Mrs. Eddy refers as "the exemplification of man's unity with God" (Science and Health, p. 18). Christian Scientists believe that in no other way can they realize the full import of what has been mistakenly regarded as the vicarious atonement of Christ Jesus, but which was in fact the perfect demonstration of man's at-one-ment with God.

Those who are familiar with the true nature of Christian Science know that it is quite unlike every form of mesmerism. It even differs from what is ordinarily referred to as "faith cure." While Jesus in his ministry often required faith of those who were seeking to be healed, and Christian Science teaches that faith is in itself a desirable quality, yet something more than the exercise of what may be termed "blind faith" is involved in the practice of true Christian Scientists. The "prayer of faith" as understood in Christian Science is in fact the prayer of spiritual understanding. This prayer is the exact opposite of that form of mental treatment which consists in the exercise of human will-power or the effort of one person to control or influence the thoughts of another by means of mesmerism or mental suggestion.

The prayer or treatment of the Christian Scientist is based upon his spiritual discernment of the fact that there is but one Mind. The mesmerist's endeavors are based upon the belief that there are minds many, and that one of these many minds can influence another for good or evil. Herein lies the danger of mesmerism or mental suggestion; whereas the safety of Christian Science practice consists in its entire dependence upon the one infinite Mind, the effect of which can be only good.

It will be seen that in depending upon the divine Mind, or God, to cast out and destroy the evils of sin and disease, the Christian Scientist is not endeavoring to hold his patient under any sort of so-called mental control. Nor is the Christian Science practitioner trying by means of thought transference or mental suggestion to change his patient's belief about sickness or disease. He is seeking through his spiritual understanding of the all-power of good to prove the unreality and powerlessness of evil,—sin, fear, disease, and death,—thereby demonstrating man's freedom from such evil suggestions. There can be no reaction or other harmful effect from such treatment. To illustrate: Suppose one raises a window shade and lets the light of day into a darkened room, he does not feel that by so doing he has changed the darkness into light; neither does he witness any conflict or strife between the light and darkness, for there is none. He merely has let the light come into the room that seemed dark and displace the sense of darkness, which is never anything more than the seeming absence of light. The activity of divine Mind in human consciousness, destroying erroneous conditions of belief, is as peaceful and harmless as the action of light coming into a darkened room and dispelling the darkness.

MIND ALONE HEALS

It would be entirely inconsistent with the Principle of Christian Science to attempt to combine its practice with the practice of medicine. To the extent that material means were employed by the metaphysician and to the extent that he compromised with matter and placed his dependence thereon, to that extent would he stultify his faith in the power of Mind as the healer of disease. By such methods the practitioner would become like the "kingdom divided against itself," which, Christ Jesus said, "is brought to desolation."

God said through Isaiah, "Come now, and let us reason together," and Christian Scientists are beginning to understand that in extending this invitation to mankind God was not asking an impossible thing. Communion with the divine Mind, which is called God, is indeed possible to one who is on this plane of existence. This has been proved by successive revelations of Truth to human kind through individuals whose spiritual perception was sufficiently clear to make it possible for them to become revelators. This succession of revelation has culminated in this age with the discovery of Christian Science, which its Discoverer says reconciles reason and revelation.

DISCOVERY AND DISCOVERER

Those who have had experience in mountain climbing will recall how, after toiling up out of the narrow confines of the canyon along the winding trails, they have finally been able to reach the very summit of the range. Having attained this exalted viewpoint, they have paused to gaze on the beauty of the panorama spread before them. There among the foothills nestles the village from which they have so lately made their way. Yonder through the valley winds the ever widening river. On the other side of the valley stretches another range of mountains, its snow-capped peaks glistening in the sunlight.

Nothing has been added to the landscape since the traveler reached the summit, but he has attained an eminence which enables him to discern that which was already there. This experience of the traveler illustrates the phenomenon of spiritual discovery. The seer and prophet in the spiritual realm becomes such because of his ability to rise in consciousness above the narrowness and limitation of material thinking to the altitude of broad, spiritual vision. Thus he attains the point of view that enables him to comprehend the facts of being and reveal them to others. He does not add to that which is, but he discerns that which always was. This describes the experience of spiritual leaders of all times.

Mary Baker Eddy did not invent anything in her discovery of Christian Science. She did not add to that which already was. She discovered the Principle underlying the spiritual healing of physical disease by the prophets, by Christ Jesus, and by the early Christians. As the result of her discovery she was able to restore to the world not only the Science of healing but the Science of being.

MRS. EDDY

Mrs. Eddy was born in Bow, N. H., July 16, 1821. She received her early education from her brother, Albert Baker, a graduate of Dartmouth College, and at the private school of Dyer H. Sanborn in Tilton, N. H. Always thoughtful and religious, she early united with the Congregational church, and remained a member of that denomination until her discovery of Christian Science in 1866. In 1875, having first demonstrated the practical worth of her discovery, she wrote and published the Christian Science textbook, "Science and Health with Key to the Scriptures." In 1879 she organized the Christian Science Church, which was later reorganized as The First Church of

Christ, Scientist, in Boston, Massachusetts. In 1881 Mrs. Eddy opened the Massachusetts Metaphysical College, the only institution of its kind having a charter from the Commonwealth. Among her published works are "Unity of Good," "Miscellaneous Writings," and other standard works on Christian Science. Mrs. Eddy established The Christian Science Publishing Society, which issues the denominational publications, including a daily newspaper, which publishes only that which is constructive and beneficial and which gives its readers a world-wide grasp of affairs.

Mrs. Eddy saw the fruition of her life-work in the extension to every part of the civilized world of the movement which she founded.

Mrs. Eddy has been declared by the Governor of her native state to have been New Hampshire's greatest woman, and truly she may be so regarded by reason of her achievements. But of all her wonderful works, that for which Christian Scientists revere and love her most is her discovery and declaration and demonstration of the life-giving truth that God is good. Therefore they say to you, "Acquaint now thyself with him, and be at peace." And for the purpose of becoming more intelligently acquainted with God as the infinitely good and loving Principle of your being, they commend you to an earnest study of

Mrs. Eddy's book "Science and Health with Key to the Scriptures."

This text-book of Christian Science is giving its students remarkable freedom from the besetments of evil, and is bringing into their daily experience the practical proof that universal good is available to mankind in every hour of need. For this they are unspeakably grateful, and because of this they are encouraged to hope and believe that you may also become students of the Scriptures in the new light thrown on them by this wonderful book, for they know that "thereby good shall come unto thee."

Printed by Libri Plureos GmbH in Hamburg,
Germany